The 9 Habits of Highly Profitable Writing

A Proven System for Earning a Full-Time Income as a Writer

Jason Brick

Copyright © 2013 by Jason Brick and Browncoat Enterprises

All rights reserved

"All rights reserved" means I own the words here and you need my permission to use them. Don't be a douche. I'm way easygoing and I like to share, but please don't go using my stuff without asking. I wouldn't borrow your toothbrush without asking, and any writer will tell you our words are way more personal than a toothbrush. So pretty please, with sugar on top, don't steal this book.

TABLE OF CONTENTS

Introduction 3
Habit 1 Write Nonfiction.. 13
Habit 2 Dress Up.. 25
Habit 3 Act Your Age 39
Habit 4 Keep Score 51
Habit 5 Write Lots 61
Habit 6 Brag... 71
Habit 7 Know Why.. 81
Habit 8 Master Your Game 91
Habit 9 Think Abundance 103
Epilogue 113

INTRODUCTION

> "We are what we repeatedly do. Excellence, then, is not an act, but a habit."
>
> —*Aristotle*

So here's the thing...

I go to writing conferences every year, all over the country. Some I speak at. Others I go to so I can learn and meet people with interests similar to my own. At every single one, I have the following conversation at least once per hour.

ME: Hi, I'm Jason.
Conference Attendee: Hi, Jason.
ME: Great to meet you.
CA: Likewise. So, Jason, what do you do for a living?

Writing is not my first rodeo. I worked in a lot of different industries before I got this gig, and I went to a lot of conventions for those industries. At martial arts conventions, the question isn't what I do for a living. It's what kind of martial art I teach to make that living. At tech conferences, people ask what technology specialty I use to feed my family. At ESL (English for Speakers of other Languages) conventions, everybody assumed that I earned my income by teaching English.

Not so at writing conferences. They're the only ones I've been to where most attendees don't make their living from the industry the conference serves. But I'm friendly, and I answer questions when people ask them. I continue the conversation.

ME: I write for a living.
CA: How?!?!?!

In a nutshell, that's what this book is about. How is it I can make a full-time living from writing while the overwhelming majority of people at writing conferences can't? Each chapter here is an attempt to answer that question.

To start with, it's the wrong question. It's wrong because it assumes something that isn't true. Other people can make a full-time living from writing. The clients I coach into writing careers generally transition within a year. The real question is subtly, but importantly different.

Why do I make a full-time living at this while the overwhelming majority of people at writing conferences don't?

What a difference a verb makes. It's not that the folks who go to writing conferences while publishing a few articles a year and working a day job can't become full-time writers if they want to. It's that they make choices that make it a bad idea.

This book is an attempt to identify some of those choices, and suggest other choices that have made it possible for me to make all the money I need from writing, instead of working a nine-to-fiver and pounding out a few words when I find the time.

My first book on writing, *Mastering the Business of Writing*, looked at the business side of those choices. It detailed the stuff I learned from successfully (and unsuccessfully!) running brick-and-mortar businesses for the first 15 years of my adult life. In here, we're look at the personal side. We'll cover concepts I discovered were important during my time in the business world, and techniques from my martial arts experience that helped me turn those concepts into habits.

I hope you find it helpful.

"There are many things that I think you can point to as proof that humans are not smart, but my personal favorite would have to be the fact that we had to invent the helmet. What was happening, apparently, was that we were involved in a lot of activities that were cracking our heads. We chose not to avoid doing these activities, but instead to come up with some sort of device to help us continue our head-cracking lifestyles."

—*Jerry Seinfeld*

How to Use This Book

Use it however you want. Read it all in one sitting, or space it out for months. Keep it on the back of your toilet. Stick it on your shelf next to writing books by Stephen King, Larry Block, Thomas Milhorn and E.B. White so you can point to that shelf and tell yourself you're serious about writing. Use it to start a fire to save your family's life the next time you're stuck in a snow storm. You paid good money for it, so you get to use it exactly the way you want to.

I never say "If I were you." I'm not anybody but me. But if I were me in your situation – the situation of somebody with writing talent who wants to become a professional writer, but doesn't know how – I would use it this way.

Step One: Read a habit a day for nine days. Give yourself time to think about what you've read and how it applies to your life right now.

Step Two: Read the epilogue and consider how to apply those ideas to building the habits you feel need the most work.

Step Three: Make a list of the things you hope to get out of a life where you write for a living. Include both general ideas like "freedom" and specifics like "I get to tell people I'm a professional writer at next year's conference."

Step Four: Reread each chapter, keeping in mind the advice on building habits from the epilogue. Apply both to the list you made in step three.

You'll come out the other side with a clear understanding of what you want out of your writing, which habits you follow already, what habits you need to build, and some ideas for how to build those habits. You won't wake up the next morning a full-fledged, full-time writer…but you will be in a better position to wake up some morning as one.

What's In This Book

The title's a pretty big giveaway. Nine chapters, each about one habit that's helped me make all the money I need from writing, working only a few hours a day, mostly from my living room with my toddler underfoot and a beer on my desk.

The 9 Habits of Highly Profitable Writing are:

Habit 1: Write Nonfiction -- Using nonfiction to make your money, even if fiction is where you passion lies. It's easier to write, easier to sell and more profitable when you sell it.

Habit 2: Dress Up -- Creating a physical and virtual appearance that will impress potential clients and make existing clients proud to recommend you.

Habit 3: Act Your Age -- Behaving like a professional even when you go to work in your shorts and last shaved the morning of your little brother's first wedding.

Habit 4: Keep Score -- Setting, managing and understanding the metrics that make your business thrive.

Habit 5: Write Lots -- Leveraging your key skill to bring in money from multiple streams, and to make each of those streams flow stronger over time.

Habit 6: Brag -- Figuring out how to tell strangers what a good writer you are, and how to turn that bragging into a steady line of new clients.

Habit 7: Know Why -- Identifying the key reasons you want to be a freelance writer for a living, instead of working a cozy, secure regular job with benefits and a janitorial department.

Habit 8: Master Your Game -- Knowing everything you can about potential clients, the publishing industry and your areas of expertise.

Habit 9: Think Abundance -- Changing your mindset about resources to make sure you always have enough time and money to write well and live the life you want.

The epilogue presents two concepts to help you build up the habits that aren't already a part of your personality. After all, this book would be pretty useless if all it did was list a set of traits you don't have and can't get.

The nine habits are an amalgam of two series of posts from my blog[1] and the comments surrounding those posts, tempered through the lens of eight years in writing and fifteen years in business. The concepts to help you build those habits come from my years as a martial arts teacher, where it's safe to say my main job was helping people build new habits.

Ready to dig in?

Good.

---

[1] www.brickcommajason.com

HABIT 1
WRITE NONFICTION

> *"Writing is writing, and stories are stories. Perhaps the only true genres are fiction and non-fiction. And even there, who can be sure?"*
>
> —Tanith Lee

This is absolutely the most important piece of advice you will ever hear about making money from your writing. It's simple, direct and to the point. In case the name of the habit didn't make it clear enough, I'll say it again:

If you want to make money writing, write nonfiction.

Why do I say that? Most people who say they want to write for a living envision turning in a novel or two a year, maybe going to a book signing or a reading in the Village every summer. Doesn't writing nonfiction defeat the whole purpose of being a writer?

I say it for about 70,000 to 100,000 reasons every year that I earn in about three hours a day. If that's not enough to convince you on its own, here are some of the facts that make those reasons happen.

1. The market is much larger. Specifically, the 2013 Writer's Market contains 412 pages of listings for magazines that buy words. Forty of those pages describe magazines that buy fiction. The other 372 are nonfiction markets.

2. The competition for that tiny fiction market is ferocious. Just about everybody has a short story or half-finished novel sitting on a hard drive somewhere. People who can write compelling nonfiction are rarer, and people who want to rarer still.

3. Nonfiction rates per word range from 5 to 10 cents to a dollar or more. Most fiction magazines want you to give them work for "exposure" or a couple of copies of the magazine so you can show your parents. Of the fiction markets that do pay, even the high-end markets top out in the 10 to 25 cents range.

4. You can take a single nonfiction idea and spin it into a dozen saleable articles without looking like a jerk.

5. Somebody has to write for businesses: marketing copy, grant documentation, technical manuals, white papers and procedure binders…at $100 or more per hour in many cases.

6. In the past few years, nonfiction books have started hitting serious best-seller, lottery winner sales. Becoming a writing millionaire is no longer just the purview of fiction writers.

7. Nonfiction is easier to write than fiction. That means you produce more words per day, with each word at a higher per-word rate.

Best of all, you can still work on your fiction in the time you're not writing nonfiction to make a living…and while you write your nonfiction, you're still exercising your writing skills. You improve your craft with every sentence you type into your keyboard.

When I talk about this at conferences, I hear a few people every time talk about how writing commercially is somehow "selling out." They seem to consider it a pedestrian sullying of their talent, something to which they could never condescend to stoop.

If that's how you want to live your writing life, go right ahead. It's a free country. But consider these two scenarios:

Scenario One: Spend two or three hours a day writing commercial copy, business documents and nonfiction articles. Spend another three hours working on your novels, poetry and short stories. Finish work two hours earlier than at a regular job, without a commute. Recharge with your friends and family, and then do it again tomorrow.

Scenario Two: Burn eight hours of every day working at Starbucks or Home Depot, then commute home and give your family the attention they need. Then find the time and energy to produce your writing in the corners of time left over.

Which of these truly "sells out" your talent as a writer? Which is more likely to mean you never finish, let alone sell, the masterpiece that's waiting inside you? It should be pretty obvious which of those two I think constitutes a crime against my writing talent.

What do you think?

> "All that non-fiction can do is answer questions. It's fiction's business to ask them."
> —Richard Hughes

Getting Started

Maybe you already have a nonfiction portfolio from going at this part time. Maybe you've been writing fiction, or just wanting to write in general, up to this point. For a detailed business plan on how to go pro in about a year, see my other book[2]. Meanwhile, I suggest you get started on the habit of writing nonfiction with these six steps.

1. Start Blogging. Create a good-looking blog and write about topics you find interesting, or about which you're knowledgeable. This gets you writing every day, and creates a portfolio of writing samples you can use to impress potential clients.

2. Go to Your Favorite Hobby Shop. Find the magazine rack. No matter how niche your hobby is, you'll find a surprising number of magazines dedicated to it. These publications pay for stories, and are typically starving for people who actually know how to write.

3. Pitch an Article to Every Magazine You Subscribe To. Or used to subscribe to. These will, by definition, be topics you're interested in and know something about. And you'll know what topics and subsections the editors like best.

---

[2] *Mastering the Business of Writing*

4. Approach Every Blog or Website You Read Regularly. Find out if they accept freelance articles or blog posts, and how much they pay for them.

5. Look at Trade Magazines that serve the industries you've worked in. Like the hobby magazines, these pay well and are usually short on people who can actually string three words together.

6. Talk to Local Businesses, especially the ones where the owner or manager knows your face. See if they need somebody to handle web copy, blogging, or document writing.

You'll get some traction in at least one of these areas if you're at all talented and professional. The demand for writing is literally bottomless, so turning that traction into a full-time career has nothing to do with luck. It only takes time, work and dedication – thing you have complete control over.

Six Ways to Screw This Up

1. Only write nonfiction for content mills that pay as little as $5 for a 500-word article. These are an okay way to get started, but you don't want to live here.

2. Limit yourself to writing in only one medium. Specialization happens later. For now, get yourself out there in as many places and ways as you can.

3. Ignore the lucrative and bountiful business and advertising markets. It's not the same as being on the cover of *Time* or *National Geographic*, but it pays the bills.

4. Write only on the topics you know about today. One of the joys of writing for a living is how many new things you learn about.

5. Refuse to write nonfiction because fiction is all you want to know. Seriously. Fiction is a lottery ticket. Nonfiction is a *meal ticket.*

6. Don't pitch the big nonfiction markets because you don't think you're "ready." Even if you're not, they won't remember your name when you finally are ready. Reach for the stars and you might get to the moon.

Six Ways To Rock This

1. Pitch a new nonfiction market every week, even if you pitch with an idea you've used before. Get in the habit of pitching often so you always have a stream of new assignments coming in.

2. Use content mills as a way to get early credentials and reliable, if low, money. It helps pay the bills during lean months, and get you in the habit of writing regularly.

3. Turn one article idea into multiple paydays by pitching variations on the theme to multiple venues. Never plagiarize yourself, but spin off new ideas to get double-duty from your research.

4. Aggressively pursue online and print mediums to put your name in front of as many audiences as possible. The longer your "Works Published" list, the better you look to potential new clients.

5. Use social media and a blog to showcase where you've been published, then keep track of the shares, likes, plusses and follows to demonstrate how effective your writing is.

6. Approach a new business every week and ask if they need freelancers to handle their writing overflow. Some of them will need you.

Advanced Habit: Your Chamber Of Commerce

Join your local Chamber of Commerce and make a habit of attending the meetings. You'll get to know local business owners, the exact decision makers you need to spend time with to get high-paying business contracts. After they get to know you, do a seminar at two meetings a year about the importance of good writing for businesses, a few tips about how they can improve their writing…and, as an afterthought, mention that you write business documents for a living.

HABIT 2
DRESS UP

> "You cannot climb the ladder of success dressed in the costume of failure."
> —Zig Ziglar

Yes, freelance writing often means you get to telecommute. Yes, that means my work day starts and ends with me in my jammies and a three-day stubble on my face. Yes, people who come to my door are lucky I'm wearing pants. Yes, this is one of the best parts of my job.

But.

You still have to maintain a professional appearance. The "face" you put forward to potential clients will determine whether or not they offer you a chance to impress them with your writing skills.

There's a story…

Wife: Honey, would you still love me if I was ugly?

Husband: If you turned ugly tomorrow – got burned in a fire, or cursed by a witch or something – of course I'd still love you. It's the parts on the inside that I fell in love with.

Wife: Awww. Thanks, honey, that's just what I needed to hear.

Husband: But if you were born ugly, I wouldn't have ever asked you out in the first place.

That's doubly, maybe triply true in the world of finding clients. If you don't show up at your best, then potential clients will never go on that first date than shows the substance behind your style. This doesn't just apply to how you personally look. The habit of dressing up means…

> **Having a professional website.** Does yours look current and professional, or like you hand-coded it using a Dummies book in 1998? Does it demonstrate that you can write coherently, and edit what you write? Does it include current contact information, and a recent resume?
>
> **Maintaining a social media presence.** Do you have a compelling profile on Google+, Facebook and LinkedIn? Does your content there compel comments, likes, shares

and +1s? Do you have a following that you can use to promote clients who hire you? Do your comments demonstrate professionalism and a positive attitude?

Using images effectively. Are all the images on your website of high quality? Do they show appropriate subject matter? Do your profiles include a photo of you looking good while doing what you do? Do you provide proper accreditation for images you didn't make yourself?

Communicating professionally. Do your emails to potential clients observe proper grammar and get your point across as effectively as possible? Do you avoid foul language in your public posts, and in your messages to clients? Do you respond rapidly to questions, and give advance warning if something happens to put you off schedule? Do you follow basic professional protocols in your communication on the phone, in person and via electronic medium?

Maintaining an impressive portfolio. Do you provide compelling and recent work samples related to the jobs you're seeking? Is there a testimonials page on your website? Do you solicit testimonials from your favorite clients once or twice every year?

Grooming yourself. Do see to basic hygiene before meeting somebody in person or via video chats? Can you put on a suit or good dress for important client meetings and initial interviews?

If you have to answer "no" to some or even most of these questions, don't panic. You've simply identified a few of the habits you need to build over the next several weeks.

Avoiding Dealbreakers

I buy groceries with the help of my toddler son. He likes identifying and counting food. I like getting the job done and spending time with him. It's a win-win. One day in line, a young woman in front of us offered her nannying services while we were both waiting at the register. A total stranger hit me up for a job, just like I tell all my writing coaching clients to do. She did a lot of things right.

- She observed the first rule of freelance job hunting: tell everybody you meet what you do, and ask them to pay you for doing it.
- She opened the conversation by demonstrating her knowledge of her field. In this case, she engaged me about parenting and her experience with children.
- She asked me for work in a straightforward, almost abrupt, manner.
- She told me about her past experience, and offered to provide references.
- Her entire communication was professional, yet approachable and friendly.

It was an excellent pitch, but I never called her. Here's why.

She was dressed in a ratty sweatshirt and very (very) tight camo pants. Sure, it was Sunday morning at the grocery store, and she even apologized for the outfit. But if you're in the game of asking for work every time you leave the house, you should dress for work every time you leave the house. It made me wonder what other details she was in the habit of forgetting.

She smelled like cigarette smoke. I don't consider this the sin a lot of people seem to think it is these days, but it is a deal-breaker for anybody who wants to spend time with my kid. My attitude on this is pretty common up here in the granola-chewing, tree-hugging, holier-than-thou Pacific Northwest. She'd neglected to do basic market research in her chosen field. That's another red flag.

Two small details of her appearance outweighed five excellent points in her favor. Remember: the people who make decisions about hiring freelancers are besieged by people asking for work. They're not looking for reasons to say yes. They're looking for reasons to say no.

Don't give them easy reasons. You should never miss out on a client just because you didn't feel like getting permission to use a photo, or put on your grownup pants on your way to get some milk. On the job, on the web, and in the world…dress up of you want to make it as a freelancer.

> *"I think that when you get dressed in the morning, sometimes you're really making a decision about your behavior for the day. Like if you put on flip-flops, you're saying 'Hope I don't get chased today.' Be nice to people in sneakers."*
> —Demetri Martin

Six Ways to Screw This Up

1. **Use unprofessional photos online, either in quality or subject matter.** Pay attention not only to your head shots and official shots, but to what's out there in social media.

2. **Violate basic protocols of communication or copyright law.** Cops have to know criminal law. Cooks have to know health codes. It's your job to know the water fish like you swim in.

3. **Talk publicly in your blog or professional social media about politics or religion.** These are the two subjects where you're likely to lose potential clients no matter what side you land on.

4. **Ignore one or more places to wear your professional face**, just because you're convinced what you have elsewhere will get you enough work. It only takes one bad choice to sour a potential client.

5. **Wait too long to get out there** because you're worried you haven't dressed up enough. Your first appearance doesn't have to be in a tux. A polo shirt and Dockers will do just fine.

6. Wait for existing clients to compliment you, rather than asking for testimonials. People like doing favors, and they'll say nicer things about you than you would dare to make up on your own.

Six Ways To Rock This

1. Get comfortable with the camera on your phone. Photo ops, either of you or to go with your blog and social media posts, are all over the place.

2. Schedule routine maintenance for your blog and social media profiles so you can update them every few months. Updated profiles, photos and news makes you look sharp and on top of things.

3. Subscribe to blogs in your areas of expertise. Engage there and share in your social media to make connections. Besides, if you're not reading in the areas where you write you don't deserve to succeed in those areas.

4. Update your resume every six months. Ditto for your testimonials and work samples page. Keep everything update.

5. Buy a good suit or business dress. Even though most of your contact will be online, you want to be prepared for the occasional in-person business meeting.

6. Create a personal social media account separate from your professional accounts to give yourself an outlet to "let it all hang out" with your friends. Even if potential clients find your personal feed, most appreciate the difference and are less likely to hold anything you say there against you.

Advanced Habit: Dress Your Work Space

Challenge yourself to clean and organize your work space at the end of each work day. This helps you feel more professional and put-together when you approach work the next morning. It also gives you a little ritual that tells your mind "hey, we're done for the day" and lets you focus on other things until it's time to go back to work.

Habit 3
Act Your Age

> *"If you think it's expensive to hire a professional to do the job, wait until you hire an amateur."*
> —Red Adair

This habit is the scourge of freelancers of all stripes, but especially of creative types like writers, web designers and artists. If writing nonfiction is the habit that's the most important, this is the one that's most commonly missing among the people I work with as a coach.

The thing about freelancers is we fired our jobs and went out on our own because we were sick and tired of being told what to do. We all thought we were smarter than our bosses, and we knew for damn sure we were better looking. We may even have been right, but do you know what we're all worse at than our old bosses?

Being a boss.

And that's where so many writers get into trouble. We're great at writing. Some of us are even good at planning long-term projects, but as a group we're pretty terrible at following through on our plans. The sad truth is that if we were good at the daily grind of getting stuff done, we'd be happy punching a clock for full-time work with benefits and paid vacation. The result of this is a host of obstacles between the average writer and the freelance income you need.

COMMON SYMPTOMS OF A THIRD HABIT DEFICIT INCLUDE:

- Turning in assignments late.
- Working until 2 in the morning to turn in something on time.
- Having no clear budget, and no solid idea of how much money you made this month
- Forgetting to invoice clients
- Showing up late
- Having to leave early
- Not sticking to a budget you create
- Slow or frustrating communication with clients
- Constant worry about if you're forgetting something
- Constant worry about money
- Having to miss family commitments to finish work
- Taking on more work than you have time for
- Finding yourself with insufficient work to fill your time
- Disorganized time
- Looking for key materials in your office, files or hard drive when you should be writing
- Taking basic requests for change personally

Don't judge yourself too harshly if you resemble the above remarks. They're epidemic among freelancers and consultants. Most of us are constitutionally challenged when it comes to professionalism and organization. The good news is this is true of nearly all of us, which means if you conquer this disadvantage by building a contrary habit, you'll have a competitive edge over all the competition who haven't.

BE POLITE

A few years back, I did a series of blog posts for a medium-sized business in Los Angeles. As we were wrapping up the deal, my client told me I beat out 150 other applicants to get the gig. I asked him if he'd mind telling me how I floated to the top of that heap. He said that 98 percent of the applicants obviously hadn't read the entire job description, done basic research into his industry, provided work samples or even bothered to spell-check their cover letters.

That goes beyond basic professionalism and into the realm of common courtesy. It's not okay to ask somebody for money while simultaneously demonstrating no regard for or interest in that person. Professionalism starts with being polite, whether it's this kind of research or simply thinking about how your decisions impact the time, stress or success of the people you do business with.

The Solution

We've established that we freelancers are bad at this, and that being bad at this keeps us from making the living we want. You'll not I don't say "the living we deserve," since maintaining unprofessional habits means we don't deserve to make any more money than we're already making.

So how do we fix it?

We find a boss.

I don't mean going back to a regular job. That defeats the whole purpose of having a freelance career. I mean find somebody who will hold you accountable for your success, and who you'll listen to when you make them kick your ass. Whoever you choose needs to be able to:

1. Make you commit to timelines and deadlines for finishing your projects.

2. Touch base with you on your progress in a way that encourages you to stay on schedule.

3. Chide you as gently or firmly as you need when you fail to keep your promises to yourself.

4. Encourage you when you don't feel like doing something important.

5. Do all of the above without the kind of drama that leads you to rebel and sabotage your own success.

When I mention this to coaching clients, a lot of them immediately think of a spouse. That's a natural idea, but in most cases it's also a mistake. There's too much emotional baggage, and too much ignoring of one another, in most marriages for this to succeed. Instead, try

A parent
A sibling
A former co-worker
A former boss
A writing group
A random friend

You can also take advantage of the burgeoning mobile worker community, which has meetups in most cities where work-from-home professionals of all stripes get together for companionship and accountability. Sometimes a like-minded stranger is a better person for giving this kind of advice than even your closest friends.

Exactly who you choose to hold you accountable is up to you, but you must have somebody. I meet weekly with a friend who owns a small motorcycle accessory business. We act as one another's accountability partners – him for my writing, me for his shop. That works for my business writing. For my fiction projects, I meet with a writing group every other week…and they give me static if I haven't delivered the chapters I promised.

> *"A professional writer is an amateur who didn't quit."*
>
> —Richard Bach

Six Ways to Screw This Up

1. Get surly with clients who take you to task for poor organization or communication. It's your job to impress them, not their job to coddle you.

2. Give up and go back to a regular job. If you decide this is what you need to be happy, more power to you…but it's not exactly rocking the freelance writing lifestyle.

3. Set up robust systems to help you be professional, but never apply them. You would be amazed how many of my clients do exactly this. It's exciting to create systems for your success. It's less exciting to live by them.

4. Say you're not capable of changing habits, that these behaviors are just a part of your core personality. That's just not true. And if it is true, it's still possible to change your core personality.

5. Convince yourself that creativity demands an unstructured environment, and clients just need to learn to live with that. Studies have found again and again that structure *breeds* creativity by giving you more abundant time and energy.

6. Overpromise and underdeliver. Hold yourself to a standard of *exceeding* both what is asked of you and what you ultimately make happen.

Six Ways To Rock This

1. Schedule your time and work each morning. A variety of studies found that 10 minutes of this each morning gives you two or more hours of extra productivity in an 8 hour work day.

2. Have accountability and planning meetings…with yourself. I make checklists at night before bed, review them in the morning, and see how many I checked off at the end of each work day.

3. Set a response timeline, and hold yourself to it. Writing those deadlines down makes a huge difference in whether or not you meet them.

4. Promise yourself you'll have an empty email inbox once a week. Seriously. I cannot overstate how good this feels.

5. Take a class, or listen to a podcast, on personal organization. Even if you're pretty organized, you'll get a new idea each week to get even better.

6. Find the best motivators to help you beat procrastination. Whatever gets you moving when it's hard, learn how to access it so Netflix or cleaning the garage don't get in the way.

ADVANCED HABIT: Just One Page (More)

Every job has assignments you hate, that you procrastinate on as if they'll go away without consequences when the deadline passes. To make yourself get on these, sit down and make yourself write just one page. In most cases, once you get rolling you'll finish two or three pages before you want to stop. This also works when you force yourself to finish one more page before stopping work for the day on a project you're getting bored with. For projects that don't measure in pages, use a time frame…ten minutes, or thirty minutes of work before you get to stop.

Habit 4
Keep Score

"What is measured, improves."

—Peter F. Drucker

We all have desires for our writing careers, whether it's making $150,000 a year from home or getting that novel published. The thing is, most writers don't make those desires real goals.

By "real goal" I mean something you've expressed in a way that's measurable and specific, attached to a time limit and written down, the check regularly.

You make it measurable so you'll know when you're done, and how much progress you've made at any given time.

You attach it to a time limit by setting a specific date by which you promise yourself you'll be finished. With large goals, it's a good idea to split it into smaller chunks along a timeline, such as writing a page a day to finish a 300-plus page book in a year.

You write it down to give the goal psychological importance and permanence. Steve Maraboli once said a goal you don't write down isn't a goal. It's a wish.

You check it regularly to keep yourself inspired, and to confirm your daily decisions and progress are in line with reaching your goals.

Keeping score is a matter of tracking your progress toward all of your goals. Metrics are how you keep score. They are ways of measuring your progress to keep yourself on track. I learned about metrics during my time running a martial arts studio. With 120 students and a staff of over 20 employees and volunteers, I had a lot of metrics to track. In my simpler life as a freelance writer, I track only a few.

1. How much money I've earned by writing.

2. How much money I've been paid for writing (sadly, not always the same as number one)

3. How many posts for my blog and social media presence I've completed.

4. How many action items – for example writing a scene or editing a chapter – I've completed on book projects.

5. How many pitches I've sent to potential clients or new magazines.

6. How many "acts of marketing" I've performed.

7. Whether or not I've completed my weekly administrative tasks.

I hold myself to specific standards for each week, and plan my weeks to make sure I reach the monthly numbers I've promised to myself. The specific numbers are tied to my needs, my schedule and what my clients are asking me to do. Over time, the individual pieces add up to success.

But only if I watch my numbers and keep them on track.

Ways To Keep Score

Really, any system that keeps your finger on the pulse of your writing business is a good system. If you already have a good handle on this, don't go looking for a new system to learn and apply. If you don't already have a system for tracking your metrics, here are a few that work pretty well.

Spreadsheets

It's possible you already use this for your family finances. Apply the same concepts to track your progress toward earning a month's worth of income, accumulating finished pages for your novel, and sending enough queries out to get the clients you want.

Paper/Whiteboard

I use whiteboards to track my daily assignments. They're easy to update as my day progresses, and they're right there on the wall to remind me to stay on task. I have a big one for my work station wall, and a little one I carry around with me. You can do the same thing on a piece of paper, a drawing pad, or whatever else suits your fancy.

Professional Software

The advantage of professional metric tracking software is it's the perfect tool for the job, fine-tunable to your exact needs and built with tools to remind you about important assignments. Some will even lock down the games on your computer if you're too close to deadline without showing sufficient progress. The bad news is these are expensive, sometimes very expensive.

Apps

Apps are the flip side of the professional software coin. They're cheap or free, but don't have the robust tools and easy customizability of the bigger suites. Still, a simple reminder app like Remember the Milk can combine with a to-do-list app to track a lot of your basic metrics.

"The success combination in business is simple. Do what you do better, and do more of what you do."

—David Joseph Schwartz

Six Ways to Screw This Up

1. **Track the wrong metrics**, focusing on numbers that don't drive the success of your writing.

2. **Check your metrics too infrequently** to make adjustments in real time. This is like trying to navigate when your GPS has a ten-minute lag.

3. **Check your metrics too often**, taking up your time without adding value.

4. **Fail to plan for the long term** in your goals and metrics. This can leave you at the mercy of market fluctuations *and* keep you pessimistic about your capabilities over the long haul.

5. **Set your short-term goals too high.** Success takes time. Give yourself that time, even when you're excited.

6. **Set your long-term goals too low.** Given time, you'll be surprised how well you can succeed.

Six Ways To Rock This

1. **Tally up your numbers every week.** Make a ritual of it, a way of telling yourself it's time to take the weekend off.

2. **Commit an hour a month to looking at your numbers** and adjusting either your expectations or your performance.

3. **Write your biggest goal in dry-erase marker on your bathroom mirror,** so you'll check it every day. While you're at it, use a post-it note on your steering wheel and a poster in front of your treadmill.

4. **Reward yourself** with something you truly enjoy to celebrate when your metrics are on track.

5. **Pay the closest attention to things you hate doing the most.** It will help make sure you get them done. Bonus points for making them the first things you do each day.

6. **Share your metrics** with your accountability partner who is willing to take you firmly to task if you repeatedly fail to keep the promises you've made to yourself.

ADVANCED HABIT: THE AUTOMATIC RAISE

Just about nobody starts a writing career making as much money as they want, and even those who do have to make more over time because of inflation. Every year, increase your expectations on key metrics. Add 10% to your income goals, or 20% to the number of people or publications you pitch. If you do that every year, you'll get that annual raise you looked forward to so much when working a regular job – and you'll be the one who decides how much it is.

Habit 5
Write Lots

> "Working hard becomes a habit, a serious kind of fun. You get self-satisfaction from pushing yourself to the limit, knowing that all the effort is going to pay off."
> —Mary Lou Retton

In Habit One, we talked about the importance of writing nonfiction if you want a career as a writer. This is absolutely true, but the truth (like all truths) is more complex than that. If you really want to make it as a writer, you need to cast a wide net of projects so you can write as much as you need to live the life you want. This takes a variety of forms.

Write For More Publications

Even as print appears to be burning out, there are thousands of magazines willing to pay you for your words. New websites appear faster than you can offer to write something for them, meaning there is an effectively infinite supply of potential clients on the web. Do the research and find out who carries articles about your areas of interest and expertise.

When you have an article idea, pitch multiple venues with slightly different angles on the same topic. Also look for tangential publications. If you're a travel writer researching a piece on museums in a local tourist town, also pitch the hobby magazines related to each museum. While you're at it, look for the kids activities at each location for an article to pitch at a local parenting magazine. This makes the most of your research, and gives you extra clips for your portfolio.

Be Willing To Write About Everything You're Offered

Don't just write about what you want. I love writing about martial arts, and I'm a regular contributor to Black Belt, the biggest martial arts magazine on the market. But my total monthly income from writing about martial arts caps out at $300 to $500. I make a living because my beat is absolutely anything somebody is willing to pay me to write. A partial list of topics I've covered recently includes travel safety, SMS marketing, social media, marriage equality, wildlife viewing, stress relief, martial arts, getting enough sleep, music for working out, feline leukemia, disability insurance, expulsion policies in private schools, student loans, virtual phone systems, drunk driving, role-playing games, search engine optimization, zombies, quantum mechanics and my toddler's bathroom habits.

I'm not an expert on everything I write about. I don't have to be, and neither do you. As a writer, your chief talents should be writing and research. As a friend I interviewed for a piece I did for

American Express OPEN Forum says, "If somebody asks you if you can do something, and you can – or you can learn how before your deadline – the answer is YES!"

Write About More Things

Make a list of 20 things you know well, or would like to learn about. For each of those things, make a list of 100 topics you could write about or research. You now have 2,000 potential articles to sell. As you do your initial work on each, you'll find at least five concepts per original idea that you can pitch to different venues. That's 10,000 total articles. At $100 each, which is low, that's $1,000,000 – a decade worth of six-figure years. And you'll come up with other ideas during that decade.

This may seem similar to just being willing to write about everything you're offered, and it is. The difference is in the impetus. Being willing to write about everything means says YES when somebody asks if you can take on an assignment. Writing about more things means coming up with as many ideas as possible to offer to potential clients. Put together, they're a powerful combination.

Write More Quickly

This is one of the biggest dividing lines I've noticed between professionals and amateurs. It's also a demonstration of why writing for a living beats writing part-time while working another job. Amateurs on web forums I frequent, and most of my clients when they come to me, talk about putting down 1,000 words on a good day. Today – not a particularly busy day for me – I'm at 7,000 with another 3,000 to go. About half of those are iterative drafts of projects, but the other 5,000 words are new content.

Let's do the math here. Even the low-paying content mill market pays about 3 cents a word. Writing 1,000 words a day means you make about $30 a day, less than $1,000 a month. Doing the same thing half as fast as I do adds up to $150 a day -$31,000 a year for working five days a week from home. And that's at the lowest end of the pay scale. At 10 cents a word, probably an average payday for commercial magazine writing, that's $2,500 a week. Writers generally get paid per word or assignment, not by the hour. The faster you work, the more you make.

Be Open to New Ideas

When I started writing, I mostly did articles for magazines and websites, but that grew to include business documentation, ad copy, even a travel guide. Then I got asked to write some scripts for video ads, then a ghostwriting assignment, then speech writing and an opportunity to publish some e-books. Every one of those gigs created a new stream of income for my writing business. It not only made me more money, it gave me a variety of types of assignment that kept me from getting bored.

I talk with a lot of writers these days, and most of them have assigned themselves some kind of niche. They might say "I'm a travel writer" or "I design brochures." That's great. Writing about our passions is one of the best parts of the job. When those people ask me why they can't make it full-time as writers, they've already answered their own question. They're violating the Fifth Habit by not writing as much as they can.

> *"Success is a function of persistence and doggedness and the willingness to work hard for twenty-two minutes to make sense of something that most people would give up on after thirty seconds."*
>
> —Alan Shoenfeld

Six Ways to Screw This Up

1. Stay away from subjects within your knowledge base because you don't like them, or don't want to do the research.

2. Eschew any given medium for displaying your work, or for finding clients.

3. Don't write when you don't feel like writing, or when you feel tired of writing for the day.

4. Commit to a project that requires contextual knowledge you don't possess, such as writing for a specialized field where you've never worked.

5. Stop writing about a topic after the first publisher buys an article.

6. Never expand how many words a day you expect yourself to write.

Six Ways To Rock This

1. Scavenge waiting rooms to find magazines you've never considered that might carry your work.

2. Keep a notebook with you at all times. Write down article and story ideas you have as they come to you.

3. Challenge yourself to find one new kind of assignment each month, or at least every quarter. Not just new topics or magazines, but new markets.

4. Cruise the low-end job boards like UpWork or Craigslist. Don't bid on those jobs, but do use it to learn what kind of writing people are buying…especially what people are buying that you're not doing.

5. Talk to other writers about what they write. There are so many ways to make a living in this industry. Nobody knows all of them.

6. Write down ten ideas for articles or blog posts every day during some of your down time.

ADVANCED HABIT: THE AUTOMATIC E-BOOK

Once you've blogged regularly for a year, take those posts and turn them into a book. It will take some rewriting, and it's considered polite to put in some new material. Use Kindle Direct Publishing, SmashWords and/or CreateSpace to put that book out there. It will give you instant credibility as a writer, and can turn into a nice stream of passive income.

HABIT 6
BRAG

> *"Marketing is too important to be left to the marketing department."*
>
> —David Packard

The truth is you have to make some sales if you want to write for a living. Professionals in every field advertise themselves, their company or both. Professional writers don't get a pass from this rule just because the concept scares most of us.

As a freelance writer, I spend about as much time marketing myself and my work as I do writing it. This includes my blog and social media presence, sending applications for contract gigs, querying publications, touching base with former clients, setting up speaking gigs, and reaching out to local businesses.

If you don't know how to market, learn. If you don't like marketing, suck it up and get to work. This is part of the freelance life, and the rewards outweigh doing something you don't love once in a while.

Every time I bring this up at a conference or with a coaching client, I hear the same objections.

"Dammit, Jason! I'm a writer, not a salesperson!"

Awesome *Star Trek* reference aside, yes you are. At least, you will have to be if you want to sell enough work to call yourself a professional writer. It's time to live reality on reality's terms.

"I don't want to sully my art with commercial concerns."

I've talked about this earlier already. You can grow your talent by writing for a living, or let that talent atrophy by giving your time and energy to another job. It's your choice

"Money's not important if you do what you love."

Karate schools don't make any real money. I lived for seven years on less than $20,000 while working 70 hour weeks doing what I loved. I did have fun, but I have a lot more fun now that I don't worry where my mortgage payment's coming from.

"I don't know how."

Yes you do. If you've ever been on a date, or gotten a job, or convinced your kid to do his homework, you have successfully sold something. You might even have enjoyed the process.

"I hate marketing."

Chances are you don't really. It's much more likely that you have a skewed perspective of what marketing really is. Even if you do hate marketing, you still have to market. The fallacy in that case isn't your belief that you hate marketing. The fallacy is your belief that it matters.

A Change In Perspective

The real secret about successful reluctant marketing is to change how you view it. Marketing doesn't have to be cheesy, manipulative "The first 100 callers get a second potato twirler absolutely free!" ad copy. Sales doesn't have to feel like the last time you bought a used car.

At its core, marketing and sales are simply identifying a need, then letting somebody know you can fill it. People need writers to write stuff. You write stuff and like money. There's a beautiful symmetry there that only needs a connection. Marketing is nothing more or less than making that connection.

Unleashing Your Geek

I'm a geek. A big geek. I dig science fiction, pay attention to comic books, appreciate the inherent mathematics in good heavy metal. I run a D&D game twice a month and have considered opinions about the differences between the book version and the movie version of Lord of the Rings.

But you know what? Everybody's a geek in their own way.

Have you ever gotten a jock talking sports statistics, or a dizzy woman who hasn't read a book since middle school talking about her favorite celebrities? What geeks! Even Mad Men lead Don Draper is a geek when he's talking about what he does best.

We're all geeks, and that's a good thing. Not long ago, I got three job offers without asking for them simply by geeking out about how awesome it is to be a writer in the 21st century. I didn't go into those conversations looking for work, or trying to make a sale. I just talked about stuff I find fascinating. My energy and passion, and the knowledge that comes from them, made the sale without me even having to try.

Don't "market" with cheap tricks and cheesy lines. Make the sale by telling people truthfully how impressive you are. If you do it well, enough people who need you will hear about you that you'll make sales without ever once having to say "Act Now!" or "Moneyback Guarantee!".

> *"You don't close a sale. You open a relationship."*
>
> —Patricia Fripp

Six Ways to Screw This Up

1. Never apply systems to your marketing. Without them, you'll never make yourself market your way into a profitable writing gig.

2. Use salesy techniques instead of creating real connections. People doing that is why I had to write a whole section on why you don't really hate sales. Don't be that guy.

3. Maintain the fiction that sales is not fun, ethically objectionable, or both.

4. Fail to track your marketing efforts or hold yourself accountable for continued marketing.

5. Tell yourself "I hate this" every time you start working on your sales and marketing.

6. Be so humble you're not willing to tell people how awesome you are.

Six Ways To Rock This House

1. Contact old and potential clients, including places you applied to unsuccessfully in the past, at least once a quarter.

2. Attend group events and networking mixers. Don't be the sales person in the room, but do talk about what you do and find out who might need you.

3. Got to conferences and conventions for businesses you know about. There are more clients there, and fewer writers.

4. Have a complete marketing plan, and get your accountability buddy to make you follow it.

5. Create a hot-shot online portfolio. Nothing kills a business faster than effective marketing that leads to a substandard product.

6. Memorize a 30-second elevator pitch about what you do and why it's important.

Advanced Habit: Breaking The Ice

The hardest part about sales for most people is making that first contact with a stranger. It's like asking somebody out on a date without the comforting hope that this one working out means you'll never have to do it again. To get over that, try out each of these tricks for one week each.

The Eye Contact Rule [3]

For one week, make direct eye contact for one to two seconds with everybody you interact with. This includes people you pass on the street. The only exceptions are situations where that might be dangerous, or where it might get you in trouble at work.

The Three Foot Rule.

Get at least 200 business cards made. For one week, never let somebody get within three feet of you without getting one and hearing your elevator pitch. No fair running away from strangers to limit the number of people who come within three feet.

After two weeks of doing both of these things, you'll find that simply approaching people who expect to be approached, then offering them services they've already bought at one time or another, isn't so bad.

---

[3] Stolen from Tim Ferris in *The Four Hour Work Week*

HABIT 7
KNOW WHY

> "Remember that everyone you meet is afraid of something, loves something and has lost something."
>
> —H. Jackson Brown Jr.

Freelancing is hard work. You set your own hours, but you have to own your time and responsibilities so you can use those hours effectively. You're your own boss, but you have to be effective at making yourself do stuff you don't want to do.

Freelance writing is even harder.

Although the demand is out there, lots of people would love to write for a living. Lots of people who would otherwise be great clients think they know how to write. That means pushing against a market that wants to pay you less than you're worth. Add to that the uncertainty of making your nut every month, the lack of health benefits or paid vacation, the fact that working from home means not going to get cart food as often as you'd like…pretty soon you start to wonder why you signed up for this gig in the first place.

And that's the reason you need to know why it's all worth it.

STARTING BIG: YOUR MISSION STATEMENT

You came to writing for a reason. It might have been simply because you like to write. It might have been because you can write from anywhere in the world, and go to work from anywhere with halfway decent Wi-Fi. It might be because of how much you hate wearing a suit to work, and Habit Two be damned. A mission statement can help you remember those reasons when things get tough.

A mission statement is a sentence or two that describes in detail why you do what you do. Most mission statements you see on corporate websites aren't actually mission statements. They're thinly veiled marketing ploys with no teeth, no heart and no meaning. Do not use them for inspiration here.

You don't want marketing speak in your mission statement. You don't need it, because this mission statement is just for you. It won't work, because you'll know if it's a load of malarkey. Instead, it should reflect exactly why you write for a living – or want to write for a living. Hopefully, it will use words that resonate with you so you keep wanting to write even on days when it's hard.

For better or worse, here is mine:

To afford what my family needs and serve my personal values while working from home with abundant time for my wife, children, friends and interests.

There's no marketing doublespeak in there. It's just a list of the key things that motivate me to do what I do. Make enough money. Be a good dad, husband and friend. Have time for my hobbies.

I love what I do, even the more challenging parts of it, but I do have rough days. When I have those rough days, I read and reread (sometimes re-reread and re-re-reread) my mission statement to keep me plugging until the days get easier again.

ZOOMING IN

Your mission statement tells you why you write in general, but what about why you write the particular piece you're procrastinating on today? That's where zooming in to a project calendar helps. It's a simple process, which itself becomes a habit as you make it part of your regular routine.

Step One: Your Five-Year Plan: Ask yourself what you want your writing career to look like in five years. How much money do you want to be making? How many books do you want in print? How about speaking gigs? Where do you want to travel? Is there a magazine you want to see your wok in? Write it all down. These are specific goals that you attach to the values you captured in your mission statement.

Step Two: Your Plan for the Year: Every six months, work out what you have to do over the next twelve months to keep yourself on track for your five-year plan. Even though you're planning a full year, you do this every six months for two reasons.

- It makes sure you always have at least six months of solid plan ahead of you at all times, instead of starting each year with no lead time.

- It lets you adjust the nearest six months of your plan according to changes in circumstance that happened since the last time you set your 12-month goals.

This adds a level of granularity, creating the steps on the path you need to follow to reach your seemingly aggressive five-year plan. After a few iterations of this, though, you'll find those five-year goals are easier to reach than you'd expected.

Step Three: Your Monthly and Weekly Tasks: Break up those yearly goals into 12 monthly sub goals, spread out to account for the rhythm of your year. Break up each month into 4 weekly plans. Those plans become daily agendas, thus creating your to-do list for the most important goals in your writing life.

When you find yourself wondering why you're writing yet another ad brochure for your local proctologist, you can trace that task all the way up the chain to your yearly and five-year plans. It will remind you that this is just one step on the path to the life you've promised yourself.

There's not much that's more inspiring than that.

"The only thing standing between you and your goal is the bullshit story you keep telling yourself as to why you can't achieve it."

—*Jordan Belfort*

Six Ways to Screw This Up

1. **Settle for a mission statement that doesn't describe your real reasons for wanting to be a professional writer.** Be bold, personal and compelling.

2. **Set monthly goals in a way that conflicts with your calendar.** For example, writers with kids should avoid heavy workloads in September and December. The start of school and the holidays make those hard months to get lots done in.

3. **Give up on your goals just because circumstances change.** Alter them to meet your new situation.

4. **Beat yourself up for missing a goal or benchmark.** It happens to everybody. What matters is how you get back on track.

5. **Fail to review your mission statement**, both for inspiration and to make sure the values it expresses are still relevant to you.

6. **Let what other people think about you become your primary motivation.** Screw those guys. Motivate yourself with what you find motivating.

Six Ways To Rock This

1. Give yourself enough time to enjoy the fruits of living the life you've designed.

2. Create a schedule for reviewing your goals and assessing your progress.

3. Rework your goals and schedule to account for new situations, including reassessing whether some goals are worth continuing to pursue.

4. Change your mission statement any time you find it no longer pushes you to succeed.

5. Forgive yourself for missing a goal. Find a way to readjust your workload to get it done soon enough.

6. Spend enough time with the people who you designed your mission statement to help you serve.

ADVANCED HABIT: ACTIVE VISUALIZATION

This one sounds little more hippy-dippy, but you'll be amazed how much it works. Spend a few minutes each morning vividly imagining exactly what your tasks for the day will lead to in the long run. Don't just daydream. Tie them directly to the long-term goals they lead to, and to the facets of your mission statement they serve. Let yourself feel the results of doing what you're about to set out to do. For what's essentially daydreaming with a purpose, this is a profoundly motivating habit.

HABIT 8
MASTER YOUR GAME

> "Research is formalized curiosity. It's poking and prying with a purpose."
> —Zora Neale Hurston

Lawrence Block is an award-winning mystery author with an immense body of work and enthusiastic following. I'm still a little mad at him for retiring, leaving me with only 10 ½ Bernie Rhodenbarr mysteries to entertain me for the rest of my life. For years, Block wrote an advice column in Writer's Digest. In one such column, he said that writers who don't read the magazines they want to write for won't get published – and they don't deserve to.

Editors I've spoken with say the same thing. You'd be amazed and appalled at how many people pitch a magazine without ever having read it, or even cruised the website. If you want to write for somebody, have the common courtesy to research what they do and who they are. Find out the kind of writing they want, their editorial slant, and what topics they're interested in publishing.

The best freelancers take it several steps further. Many sites and magazines have editorial calendars that describe in broad strokes what kinds of articles they've already slated for a specific issue, and any special topics they want to cover at certain times of the year. They'll also tell you early they need to receive a piece in order to have it ready for a specific issue. This research lets you pitch your ideas form an angle based on what the magazine has already decided to cover.

The same goes for business writing. If you approach a business, approach already knowing what kind of copy they have on their website and in their advertising. Come prepared with specific examples of how you can make it better. Have the common courtesy to know a little bit about that prospective client before you ask them to give you money.

Researching Opportunities

Researching what specific venues you want to write for is vital, but you won't get far without also researching all the various venues that might carry your work. There are so many fish in the writing market sea there's no way you know about them all, let alone which ones are currently in need of your particular writing skill set. Consider this list.

Professional blogging for business
Writing your own blog for sales or advertising
Microbusiness/niche blogging
Developing business documents
White papers
Technical writing
Grant writing
Business plans
Venture capital proposals
Nonfiction articles for major magazines
Nonfiction articles for trade and hobby magazines
Ghostwriting
Advertising collateral
Web copy
Legal SEO
Informational SEO
Social media releases
Press releases
Local newspapers
Regional newspapers
Ebooks
Self-published books
Direct mail marketing copy
College entry essays
Traditional publishing
Case studies
Speeches
Resumes

These are all markets that pay real money for good words. The top tier on most pay a dollar or more for each word you produce. Thousands of professional writers derive their sole income from writing in just one of these categories.

The deeper you research your market and industry, the more opportunities you'll find to sell your work. That means more assignments, and more money.

KNOWING YOUR RATES

One reason people get discouraged about writing for a living is they see ads for gigs that pay $5 for 1,000 words or some similarly ridiculously low fee. Though the price for any work ultimately comes down to what you negotiate, I see four distinct tiers of payment in most circles.

Insulting

Some publishers or clients want to pay $5 or less for a blog post or article, or they want you to write for free to get exposure for your work. Do not accept offers at this price point. You'll make less than minimum wage. Worse, accepting those offers perpetuates the idea that this is a reasonable amount to pay for what we do.

It's okay to write for trade, for example doing some blog entries at your kid's karate school in exchange for a few private lessons, but that's not working for free. It's exchanging value for value...which is what professionals do.

Breaking In

A wealth of writing opportunities pay between 3 and 6 cents a word. A lot of it is with content mills or low-end legitimate publishers. It's not what you deserve, but can still add up to a decent living. If you take 30 minutes to write 1000 words, that's still $30 to $60 an hour. Not a bad payday.

Until you get good at estimating and negotiating your contracts, you'll probably also spend many of your first hourly assignments stuck making about this much per word. The per-word rate will get even lower as you become better at your craft. That's why writers negotiate on a per-job basis instead of a per-hour contract.

Professional

A portfolio of strong copy coupled with good testimonials will land you jobs where you get $60 to $150 for a single blog or online article. You'll also start to get assignments with mid-range national publications for about the same amount per word. At this rate, it's possible to clear six figures a year if you're willing to make a real job of it. I work mostly in this tier, and make a solid middle-class living while working about three to four hours on most weekdays.

Elite

I've completed about a dozen assignments at this tier, and would love to do more. Rates of $1 to $1 per word for articles of several hundred or thousands of words are the norm here. Major national magazines, ghostwriting for major clients and a few top online publishers pay these rates. You'll also get paid at this level for short, high-impact work like brochures or direct mail scripts – though you'll find they words take longer to write for those assignments.

> *"Never become so much of an expert that you stop gaining expertise. View life as a continuous learning experience."*
>
> —Denis Waitley

Six Ways to Screw This Up

1. Forget to check the "last updated" note on a website or submission guidelines page when researching editorial information.

2. Trust your existing expertise without checking resources to update your knowledge. It's easy to get caught with your pants embarrassingly down.

3. Work for free. Know your worth, and never work for less than that.

4. Fail to reach for higher tiers of earning just because your portfolio doesn't look like David Quammen's or Malcolm Gladwell's.

5. Get complacent about doing just one kind of writing, without researching what other opportunities are trending and hot.

6. Pitch a new customer knowing nothing about their needs. It's rude to ask somebody for money without doing the courtesy of a little research.

Six Ways To Rock This

1. Challenge yourself to find at least one new kind of assignment each month, preferably one that pays more than you're used to charging.

2. Create a database with relevant information about each publication or client you pitch. Use the format to help you know what info you need to find on new prospective clients.

3. Remind people who ask you to work for free that you're a professional, and professionals get paid.

4. Read the editorial guidelines and editorial calendars of magazines. Farm them for article ideas.

5. Read at least one blog post a day about the business of writing, or your field of expertise.

6. Follow thought leaders in your industries on social media to get the gist of what changes are coming.

ADVANCED HABIT: SIT AT THE GROWNUP TABLE

Whenever you're at a function for any industry, find the "grownup table" at any mixer or sit-down meal. It's where the top-level people in attendance, along with the people who organized the event, will be. Since it's your job to know about what's going on, and who's making it happen, go join that conversation. Act like you belong there. In most cases, so will everybody else. There's no such thing as a shortcut to success in writing, but this is a pretty good way to jump ahead a few slots in the queue.

Habit 9
Think Abundance

> "Start with big dreams and make life worth living."
> —Stephen Richards

Write Nonfiction is the most important habit for giving you the opportunity to make a good living as a writer. This last habit, though, is the most important for seizing that opportunity. It's the difference between wanting to write for a living and actually writing for your daily bread.

Thinking abundance is the opposite of thinking scarcity, which is what most writers I work with do when I meet them. Most writers have the following monthly earning cycle:

1. Write your butt off.
2. Count up how much money you made.
3. Spend that money.
4. Repeat.

It's easy to fall into that rut, and the rut feels safe while you're in it. However, it means you're making only as much money as you happen to make. It's no way to grow a freelancing business, and no way to meet those five year goals from Habit Seven. Perhaps worse, you never feel done writing for the month, or the week, or the day. There's no "off" button because you haven't defined a finish line.

Instead, consider the power of a different monthly earning cycle:

1. Identify how much money you want.
2. Figure out how much writing you must do to make that much money.
3. Write that much.
4. Stop writing.
5. Spend the money.
6. Repeat.

This is thinking abundance. Instead of asking "Can I afford what I want?" you ask "What must I do to afford what I want?" It gives you control of how much you make from your freelance career, which means it lets you live exactly the life you want by writing for a living.

Abundant Time

You can apply the abundance mindset to your time just as easily. When working a regular job, sometimes you have to be at work instead of going on vacation or seeing your child's recital. When freelancing with a scarcity mindset, things get even worse. You skip all kinds of things you want to do because you feel like you have to work all the time.

Instead, apply the question "What must I do to get to do what I want?"

Want to coach your kid's soccer team every Tuesday and Thursday evening? Schedule a little extra work on Monday and Wednesday night, or on Saturday morning before everybody gets up. Want to take a two week vacation? Spend two months doing an extra assignment a week until you've amassed enough saving to not have to work while you're away. You never have to ask anybody for permission, and there's no limit to the flexibility of your time…as long as you plan for it and commit those extra hours.

On the back end, this is how regular jobs figure vacation time. You get paid more than you salary for each day you work, and that extra pay gets applied to some time you don't come to work in the future. That's exactly like working harder for a day so you can take another day off. The only difference is when you freelance with an abundant mindset, you're the one in control of how much, how often and when you get to do that.

The Fine Print

Thinking abundance is a simple change with broad benefits for your lifestyle and income as a writer. However, there is one point where you should always maintain a scarcity mindset: when you're actually spending money.

Planning to earn how much you want to spend is great, and it will work more often than it doesn't. Just don't spend that money until you see it in your bank account. Spending those dollars before they hatch creates debt, which makes it that much harder to earn what you need to do what you want.

Six Ways to Screw This Up

1. Limit your long-range financial goals to what you're able to earn right now.

2. Don't check your weekly progress toward your monthly earnings goals.

3. Focus your mind on what you can't afford. Focus on how you will reach a space where you can afford it.

4. Confuse abundance with extravagance by buying what you don't need to impress people you don't care about.

5. Never save money against months when your plan just doesn't work out.

6. Remain in a scarcity mindset because it's comforting and safe.

Six Ways To Rock This

1. Ratchet up your earnings goals every few months to gradually expand what's reasonable for what you want.

2. Cut out nonessential expenses so you have more disposable funds to make life more fun to live.

3. Apply abundance to every finite resource in your life. Resources aren't hard to get if you know how to work for them.

4. Be willing to work hard to reach your goal.

5. Apply the accountability systems from Habit Four to your earning potential.

6. Take at least four short vacations every year. These keep your energy up and give your creativity a boost.

ADVANCED HABIT: THE ONE MONTH CHALLENGE

One month out of the year, challenge yourself to make twice what you usually ask yourself to earn with your writing. Even if you don't reach that goal, you'll probably be surprised how much you do earn. That little bonus will be nice to spend on reducing debt, increasing savings, or just spoiling the people you love. Better yet, it will put you in the habit of a new assumption about what you're capable of accomplishing.

"There is a lie that acts like a virus within the mind of humanity. And that lie is, 'There's not enough good to go around. There's lack and there's limitation and there's just not enough.'
The truth is that there's more than enough good to go around. There is more than enough creative ideas. There is more than enough power. There is more than enough love. There's more than enough joy. All of this begins to come through a mind that is aware of its own infinite nature."

—*Michael Beckwith*

Epilogue
Outroduction

> "A man who can't bear to share his habits is a man who needs to quit them."
> —Stephen King

I mentioned earlier that I'm a martial artist. In fact, I'm a sixth degree black belt with thirty years of training experience. Becoming a black belt isn't about memorizing a series of tricks, even though many of the tricks you get to learn along the way are both fun and effective. It's about developing habits of movement, habits of awareness, and habits of worldview that make me a happier, safer and (hopefully) better person.

The same is true of this book. Yes, I've included a handful of tips and techniques I hope you use in your writing career starting right now. They've helped me and I don't mind sharing, but they won't help you if you approach them with a "one and done" attitude. This book isn't about that. It's about developing habits that make you a happier, more effective and more affluent writer.

Building habits can be tricky. It takes time, effort and a willingness to see yourself fail. Though there's no one prescription for successfully turning behaviors into habits, here are two approaches I've seen work for many of my clients.

ABUNDANT TIME

This is a metric (remember metrics?) for developing individual habits. The first thing you do is identify six habits you want to develop. Don't use broad descriptions like the titles of the habits in this book, but instead drill down to specific behaviors that feed those broader categories. It's completely okay to have multiple behaviors that support one larger general habit.

For example, let's say I want to improve my communication and get more assignments. From those two broad goals, I identify six behaviors. Five are from those goals, and the sixth is based on a request from my family.

1. How many magazine articles I pitch
2. My social media interaction
3. My progress on the book I'm writing
4. Paying attention to my wife
5. My response time with emails.
6. How well I keep track of old clients.

I think about my priorities, and what's reasonable for my time, and I set five of them in a 5-4-3-2-1 pyramid that I commit to meeting each workday.

5 interactions on social media
4 breaks to talk with my wife
3 emails to check in with old clients
2 pitches to new magazines
1 new lead for assignments

The final point on the pyramid addresses the sixth goal, but expresses it as a negative.

0 emails in my inbox at the end of the work day

This system lets you build habits by making a specific level of commitment to new behaviors in a way you measure daily. As different habits become part of your routine, you can swap them out for a new behavior you want to add.

"Your beliefs become your thoughts. Your thoughts become your words. Your words become your actions. Your actions become your habits. Your habits become your values. Your values become your destiny."
—*Mahatma Ghandi*

The 20-Day Challenge

If you ask thirteen experts, you'll get thirteen different answers about how long it takes to change a behavior into a habit...but the mean falls around the three week mark. A 20-day challenge builds habits by capitalizing on that.

The concept is simple. Choose something you want to make part of your regular routine. Commit to doing it every day for the next 20 days, and then do it come hell or high water. I find this works because 20 days isn't much of a hardship. You can do pretty much anything for 20 days in a row if you really want to. It also makes building that new habit less intimidating, again because three weeks is doable. Once the 20 days are up, you can let yourself skip a day if you need to...but you probably won't because the behavior will have become a part of your routine.

You can also do a 20-day challenge in reverse by choosing to eliminate a behavior for 20 days. In my personal life, this has been the absolute best technique for quitting my self-destructive habits. Just like with building routines, the time frame is short enough to be reasonable but long enough to fundamentally change your habits.

It's important to time the 20-day challenge right. Don't schedule it if you're going to have major obstacles during the 20 days, such as the holiday season, a major assignment or visiting in-laws. This process can be hard, and you'll need all your personal resources to succeed. Schedule it for a period when you have 20 consecutive days of reasonably smooth sailing.

Other Books by Jason Brick

Books on Writing

<u>Writing is Serious Business</u>
Build Your Writing Platform in 12 Months

The Farkas Foxtrots

Child's Play
Train Wreck
Wingman
Safe Word
Wake-Up Call
Clusterfuck

THANK YOU FOR READING

If you enjoyed this book or found it useful, I'd be very grateful if you'd post a short review on Amazon. Your support really does make a difference, and I read all the reviews personally so I can get your feedback and make this book even better.

If you'd like to leave a review then all you need to do is click the review link on this book's page on Amazon here: http://amzn.to/158qTUJ

Thanks again for your support!

About the Author

Jason's favorite part of writing professionally is getting to do his job wherever he wants, whenever he wants. It lets him be the kind of dad and husband his family deserves. He has written over 5,000 articles for print and online publications, and speaks nationally to businesses about writing, and to writers about business. He works internationally coaching writers in various fields on how to have as much fun with their writing as he has with his.

When not writing, Jason practices martial arts, plays tabletop games and works hard at spoiling his wife and kids. He also writes fiction in the young adult and crime genres.

Contact Jason at brickcommajason@gmail.com, or read his blog at brickcommajason.com.

> *"A man is like a novel: until the very last page you don't know how it will end. Otherwise it wouldn't be worth reading."*
> —*Yevgeny Zanyatin*

ACKNOWLEDGMENTS

> "No man is an island, entire of itself. Every man is a piece of the continent, a part of the main."
> —John Donne

If you write at all, like most people who read this book probably do, you already know that a complete list of people to thank will be longer than the book itself. An incomplete list has to include

My Family

My parents, grandparents, wife, children and assorted family – whether or not they actually share my DNA – who loved me and didn't laugh even once when I said "I want to be a writer."

Mentors

It's impossible to overstate how helpful somebody who's been there before can be, or how much I appreciate their willingness to help me learn from their mistakes. Kathy Fisher, Jack Rochester, Bill Packer, Linda Needham, Julie Fast, Tom Callos, John Ellis, Lee Sprague.

Inspirations

The difference between an inspiration and a mentor is like the difference between a stalker and a girlfriend. You have a similar relationship with both, but only one of them knows about it. David Quammen, Ray Bradbury, Lawrence Block, Joe R. Lansdale, Jim Butcher.

And of course, again to my wife and sons. Everything I do is for you. This is no exception.

Made in the USA
Columbia, SC
02 August 2019